Page Formatting

EASY WORD ESSENTIALS 2019

BOOK 2

M.L. HUMPHREY

ISBN: 978-1-63744-060-5

SELECT TITLES BY M.L. HUMPHREY

WORD ESSENTIALS 2019

Word 2019 Beginner

Word 2019 Intermediate

EASY WORD ESSENTIALS 2019

Text Formatting

Page Formatting

Lists

Tables

Track Changes

CONTENTS

Introduction

The *Easy Word Essentials 2019* series of books is designed for those users who just want to learn one specific topic rather than have a more general introduction to Microsoft Word 2019, which is provided in *Word 2019 Beginner* and *Word 2019 Intermediate*.

Each book in this series covers one specific topic such as formatting, tables, or track changes.

I'm going to assume in these books that you have a basic understanding of Microsoft Word. However, this book does include an appendix with basic terminology just in case I use a term that isn't familiar to you or that isn't used the way you're used to.

This entire series of books is written for users of Word 2019. If you have a different version of Word then you might want to read the *Easy Word Essentials* series instead which is written as a more general approach to learning Microsoft Word.

For most introductory topics there won't be much of a difference between the two, but just be aware that this particular series does not worry about compatibility with other versions of Word whereas the more general series does.

Also, just a reminder that the content of this book is directly pulled from *Word 2019 Beginner* and/or *Word 2019 Intermediate* so there may be references in the text that indicate that.

Alright. Now that the preliminaries are out of the way, let's dive in with a discussion of page formatting, including how to use breaks and add page numbering, headers, and footers.

Page Formatting

If you're going to print a document that is more than one page long, chances are you'll want to add page numbering to the document as well as maybe a header or footer that includes the document title or your name or both. Let's talk about how to do that.

Page Numbering

First, do not ever manually number your pages. Word will do this for you. By letting Word do this, you ensure that the page numbering will still work even when you make edits to the document.

Nothing worse than putting a 1 at the bottom of what you think is page one and then deciding to add a title to the document and suddenly there's a random 1 in the middle of the second page.

So don't do that. Please.

(Says the person who has occasionally been stuck fixing a document where someone did in fact do this. That and the person who manually formatted the text to *look* like track changes...Took me ages to realize what that person had done. And even longer to fix it. But you're reading this book so you won't do that kind of thing, right? Right.)

To add page numbers to your document, go to the Header & Footer section of the Insert tab which is towards the right-hand side, and click on the arrow next to Page Number.

This will bring up a dropdown menu that lets you choose where on the page you want your page numbers to display. If you hold your mouse over those options, you can then choose how you want those page numbers to look.

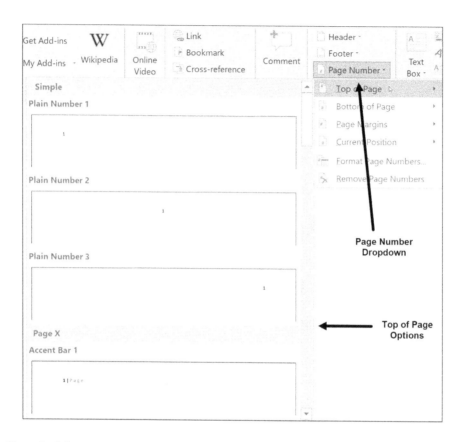

Above I've held my mouse over Top of Page and you can see the first four options I have to choose from, left, middle, right, and a left-hand accented option. If I scroll down in that list there are actually twenty-five total options to choose from some of which are quite distinctive.

Click on the choice you want and Word will insert it into the header (for top of page) or footer (for bottom of page). If you choose the page margins options, that is inserted into a standalone text box on the side of the page.

Current Position will insert the page number where your cursor currently is, so I'd only use that one if you already have a header or footer in your document (or a text box you want to use) and you're clicked into that space.

The Format Page Number option in that dropdown can be used to change the numbering format (to small case Roman numerals for example), the starting page number, or to specify that the numbering should or should not continue from a prior section. (This becomes much more relevant when you have sections in your document that require separate numbering. I cover how to create sections in *Word 2019 Intermediate*.)

For a basic simple page number using the dropdown menu and choosing one of the defaults should really be all you have to do.

Headers and Footers

Inserting a page number is basically a specialized version of inserting a header or footer. When you insert the page number at the top of the page or the bottom of the page Word creates a space that is separate from your main text and puts the page number there. But you can also put other text into the header or footer like your name or the title of the document.

Doing so will repeat that text at the top or bottom of the page for the entire document. (Or section if you're using sections. Also, you can set it up so that alternating pages have different text in them like a book does. But for basic headers and footers it repeats throughout the document.)

A header goes at the top of your page.

A footer goes at the bottom of your page.

To add one, go to the Header & Footer section of the Insert tab and click on the arrow below the one you need (header or footer), and then choose the option that works best for you, just like you did with page numbering.

Just like with page numbering you will have various pre-formatted options to choose from like these three for the footer:

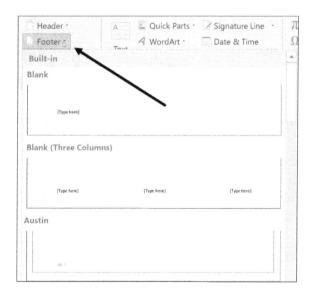

You're not stuck with the format you choose. For example, with short story submissions, they usually want the header to be in the top right corner. If you choose the Blank header option, that creates a header that's in the top left corner. But you can simply go to the Home tab and choose to right-align the text in your header and that will put it in the right corner instead.

After you choose your header or footer option, Word creates a header or footer and inserts [Type here] into the designated spots where you're supposed to put text.

To edit that text, just start typing because it will already be highlighted in gray. If it isn't highlighted in gray, select the text and then start typing.

Text in your header or footer works just like text in your document. You can use the same options from the Home tab to change your font, font size, color, etc.

As mentioned above, headers and footers are in a separate area from the main text of your document. If you're in a header or footer and want to go back to the main document, you can (1) double-click back onto the main body of your document, (2) click on Close Header and Footer in the menu bar which should be showing in the Design tab under Header & Footer Tools, or (3) hit the Esc key on your keyboard.

If you're in your main document and want to edit your header or footer, you can (1) double-click on the text in the header or footer, or (2) right-click on the header or footer and choose "Edit Header" or "Edit Footer" from the dropdown.

Margins

Margins are the white space along the edges of your document. The default margins in Word 2019 are one-inch margins all around which is pretty standard so you probably won't have to edit this often.

But if you need to edit your margins, you can go to the Layout tab and under the Page Setup section click on the dropdown under Margins. This will give you the choice of Normal, Narrow, Moderate, Wide, Mirrored, Office 2003 Default, and Custom Margins.

Mirrored margins are for printed texts where the inside margins are the same for facing pages and the outside margins are the same for facing pages. (As opposed to thinking about the left-hand margin and the right-hand margin which is what you think about with a report or other printed document that is seen one single page at a time.)

Each option, except Custom Margins, shows what the margins are for that option.

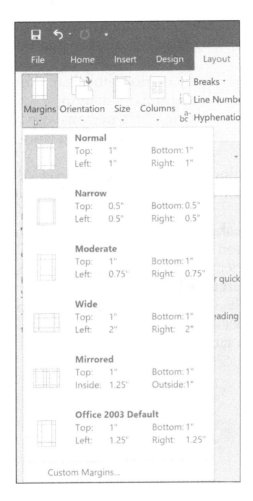

Clicking on Custom Margins, will open the Page Setup dialogue box directly onto the Margins tab. You can also open the Page Setup dialogue box to the Margins tab by clicking on the expansion arrow for the Page Setup section.

This lets you specify a custom value for each margin as well as for the document gutter. (Which matters if you're printing book-style.) In the Pages section dropdown you can also specify that the margins should be mirrored.

Page Orientation

A standard document has a page orientation of portrait. That's where the long edge of the document is along the sides and the short edge is across the bottom and top. This is how most books, business reports, and school papers are formatted, and it's the default in Word.

But sometimes you'll create a document where you need to turn the text ninety degrees so that the long edge is at the top and bottom and the short edge is on the sides.

A lot of tables in appendixes are done this way. Also presentation slides are often this way. That's called landscape orientation.

(Think paintings here. A drawing of a person—a portrait—is generally taller than it is wide. A drawing of a mountain range—a landscape—is generally wider than it is tall.)

To change the orientation of your document, go to the Page Setup section of the Layout tab, click on the arrow under Orientation, and choose the orientation you want.

If you use section breaks--which are covered in *Word 2019 Intermediate*—you can set the page orientation on a section-by-section basis. But if you're not using sections, changing the orientation on any page will change the orientation of the entire document so be careful with this one.

You can also change the orientation in the Page Setup dialogue box which can be opened via the expansion arrow for the Page Setup section. The orientation option is on the Margins tab directly below the Margins settings.

Breaks

Breaks are another incredibly useful tool. They allow you control over a complex document so that you can specify exactly where each page should start, for example, as well as create different sections within a document that have different headers, footers, page numbering, page orientation, etc.

Never, and I repeat, never, should you use "Enter" in a document to get to the next page to start a new section or chapter. Do not do that. Use a page break instead.

Because think what happens if you change the font or font size or make edits in your document. Suddenly those ten enters you used are too many or too little and you end up with your Corporate Summary heading at the bottom of the page instead of the top where it belongs. And fixing that little issue may then lead to having to fix others.

Page breaks solve that issue and even as your text adjusts, they still do what they need to which is make sure that your next section starts where it should.

I have also worked at companies that created each section of a report as a separate document and then saved one final version of the whole thing as a merged PDF.

But that approach requires a lot of manual effort to keep the page numbering consistent across files, for example, and is much more prone to error. Far easier to use a section break to let Word know that this portion of a document is different in some crucial way from other sections of the document.

So. Page breaks and section breaks:

Learn them. Love them.

They are fantastic.

Basics

Breaks can be found in the Page Setup section of the Layout tab. If you click on the dropdown menu under Breaks, you'll see that there are multiple options to choose from.

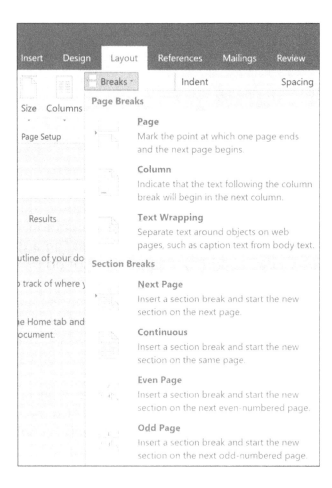

The two main sections are for Page Breaks and Section Breaks, which we'll define in a moment.

You can also insert a basic page break via the Pages section of the Insert tab or by using Ctrl + Return.

Page Breaks

Let's start with page breaks. Page breaks insert a break in your document so that your text moves to the next page or column, as the case may be, regardless of how much space is left on the page.

Page

The first option under Page Breaks is Page. This option ends the text on the current page at the point where the break is inserted and continues that text at the top of the next page.

Before you insert a page break, be sure to position your cursor at the end of the text (or image as the case may be) right before where you want the break.

For me this is usually the end of the last line of the last paragraph on the page.

Then you can use either Ctrl + Return or go to one of the Page break menu options and insert your page break.

When you do this, Word will move everything past that point down so that the next line of text (or image) starts at the top of the next page.

A page break can be useful for when you don't need to edit the header, footer, or page numbering, but you do need whatever comes next to move to the next page. For example, a chapter start or section start in a report or document where the header and footer are going to remain the same throughout the document.

(Sometimes when I insert a break, Word will stretch out the last line of text in that last line of text as if trying to justify it. If that ever happens to you, just click at the end of the line and hit enter. It'll move the page break to the next line and fix the text back to your normal formatting.)

Column

Column breaks come into play when you have your text formatted into multiple columns (which we'll discuss later).

A column break allows you to make sure that text you want in a specific column appears in that column.

To insert a column break, click into the text in your document at the point where you want the new column to start and then choose the Column break option under Page Breaks.

All text from that point forward will move to the next column.

Section Breaks

Section breaks are essential for when you want to use a different header, footer, page numbering, page orientation, or number of columns between different portions of your document.

Section breaks are what I use for breaks between chapters in a book where I have a blank left-hand page before my chapter starts. I also use them in all books to separate my front matter from the main body of the document so that I can have the proper page numbering in my books.

Another use for them would be in a report where the header in each section of the report needs to be different. Or where an appendix needs to be formatted using landscape orientation.

There are four types: Next Page, Continuous, Even Page, and Odd Page.

Next Page

The Next Page section break will insert a break and start the next section on the next page. So it's basically like a page break except that you can make changes to the section and not have them carry through to the whole document. (We'll talk about intermediate-level use of headers and footers next and discuss there how to combine a section break with different headers, footers, or page numbers across sections.)

It works just like page breaks. Go to the last line of the last paragraph for the prior section and then choose Next Page from under Section Breaks in the Breaks dropdown menu of the Page Setup section of the Layout tab.

Word will move everything from that point forward to the next page and will label that as a separate section of the document.

A next page section break and a standard page break will look exactly the same until you make changes to the header, footer, or page formatting.

Continuous

A continuous section break will not move the text to the next page but will separate the text on that page into separate sections.

The only time I can think I would use this one is if I had multiple paragraphs of text that I want to be in multiple columns on the same page with other text either before or after it that I wanted in a single column.

With columns, which we'll discuss later, you can format a single paragraph to have multiple columns by selecting that specific text first. But if you want to apply columns to multiple paragraphs at once, the easiest way is to click into that section of your document and change the number of columns for the whole section at once.

Even Page/Odd Page

The final two options are the Even Page and Odd Page section break options. The Even Page option will split the document at the point of the section break and will start the next section at the top of the next even-numbered page. The Odd page option will split the document at the point of the section break and start the new section at the top of the next odd-numbered page.

Theoretically these are even better than the Next Page option for something like a report or a book where you want each section or chapter to start on the right-hand side of the page, especially the Odd Page option.

But do be careful with this one. In prior versions of Word it has worked inconsistently for me. I've tested it in Word 2019 and it seems to be fine, but definitely double-check your document to make sure that all of your sections do in fact start on the even-numbered or odd-numbered page as you specified.

(The last time this gave me problems my current Odd Page section break looked like it was working just fine, but when I looked back at other Odd Page section breaks I'd added they had reverted to plain Next Page section breaks.)

Remove a Page or Section Break

If you ever need to remove a page or section break, you can just go to the end of the first section and use the delete key or go to the beginning of the next section and backspace. I usually use the delete option.

You don't need to see your page or section break to do this, but if you want to see your page or section break, you can click on the paragraph mark on the top right of the Paragraph section of the Home tab to show all breaks in the document.

A page or section break on its own line will show as a dotted line or two dotted lines across the page with Page Break or Section Break in the middle of the dotted line.

Sometimes if a page or section break is on the last line of a paragraph and not on its own line it won't be visible even if you have paragraph marks set to show. It will just appear as a few small dots at the end of the line if the text in that line takes up too much of the space.

A continuous section break is similar except it will be labeled Section Break (Continuous). Same for a column break which is labeled Column Break.

You can usually identify breaks by the way the text behaves where the break has been inserted since the text will move to another page for no apparent reason. (Although someone using Enter multiple times can get the same effect, so be careful.)

Headers and Footers (Intermediate Version)

Now that we've covered breaks let's revisit the topic of headers and footers, particularly some more advanced options for using them.

As a refresher, to insert a header, footer, or page number, you can do so by going to the Insert tab and choosing Header, Footer, or Page Number from the Header & Footer section. Each option has a dropdown menu with a number of various style choices.

To access a header or footer that you've already inserted into your document, you can simply double-click on that space. If that doesn't work, you can also right-click on the space and choose Edit Header or Edit Footer as the case may be.

To exit a header or footer and return to the main text of your document, you can use Esc or double-click in the main space of the document.

* * *

Alright. Now that we've covered those basics, let's talk about some fancier ways to format headers and footers, starting with changing your settings so that the first page of your document has a different header, footer, or page number than the rest of the document. (Very useful for printed reports or short story submissions, for example.)

Different First Page Header/Footer/Page Number

If you open most books you'll see that there isn't a header on the first page of any chapter. It's blank. But then the rest of the chapter does have a header.

And if you have a report with a cover page, chances are you don't want a header on that cover page. So how do you do this? How do you set it so that your first page has a different header or footer than the rest of your pages?

First, insert a header. If you've already done that, open the header.

In the menu bar above your document you should see a Design tab at the end of the listed tabs with the label Header & Footer Tools above it. Like this:

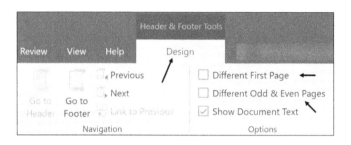

In the center of the choices under that tab is the Options section, pictured above on the right-hand side.

The first row of that section says Different First Page and has a checkbox. By default this option is not checked. But if you want a different first page header and/or footer for your document, you can check it.

Checking that box separates both the header *and* footer of the first page so that any edits made on that first page are exclusive to that page and any edits made in the header or footer in the rest of the document don't impact the first page.

Once you check that box you can delete the header on the first page and the header on all of the other pages will remain untouched, for example.

Since I generally want my footer on the first page to look the same as the rest of the document, I only check this box after I've finished all of my formatting. That ensures that the footers across my document are identical.

(I will add here that you shouldn't worry if it takes a few tries to get your headers and footers throughout your whole document looking the way you want them to. Especially when you start messing with different first page headers or, what we're about to talk about, different odd and even page headers. Also, different sections. I've been doing this for years and I still make mistakes. Remember Ctrl + Z (Undo) is your friend and there's not much that you can do wrong in Word that can't be fixed.)

Different Odd and Even Pages

Another choice you have in the Options section of the Header & Footer Tools Design tab is Different Odd & Even Pages.

I don't recall ever using this with a business report or school paper, but I use it for every single book I format. Pick up a book from your shelf and you should see that for every chapter the author name is on one page and the title or chapter name is on the opposite page. It's a rare book that's formatted differently than that.

So, how do you do this?

First, insert your header or footer.

Next, click on Different Odd & Even Pages in the Options section of the Header & Footer Tools Design tab.

Nothing will change immediately. Your header and footer will still look exactly like they did before, but now if you make a change to the header or footer ion an odd-numbered page it will only impact your other odd-numbered pages. Same for even-numbered pages.

(This all gets really fun when you have different headers and footers for first pages and then different headers and footers for odd and even pages because sometimes you have to go back three pages to find another page that has the same header and footer as the one you're working on.)

Headers and Footers and Section Breaks

The choices we just discussed allow for some pretty sophisticated formatting without ever requiring a section break. But if you have any blank pages in your document (say between chapters or sections) or if you need to have different headers or footers (say in an appendix or your front matter where you want a different page numbering or page numbering style), then you're going to need to combine the use of headers and footers with the use of section breaks.

The nice thing about Word is that it will default to continuing your page numbering when you insert a section break. This means that, for example, if you have multiple chapters in a document you don't have to worry about changing the page numbering settings every single chapter.

But there are going to be times that you do need to change your page numbering between sections. For example, between the table of contents in a report and the main content of the report.

Generally, you should use lower case Roman numerals (i, ii, iii, etc.) for the pages that contain the table of contents and use standard numbers (1, 2, 3, etc.) for the main body content. (Weirdly enough, you actually continue the standard numbers if you have any additional content at the back of the book and want to number those pages.)

Okay, so how do you do this?

I'm going to assume that you already have sections breaks in your document because this option is only available if there are already multiple sections.

The first step is to unlink one section from another. To do this, click into the header or footer of the first page where you want to see the change.

So if I have a table of contents and then the main body of a report, I'd go to the header or footer of the first page of that main body of the report.

If I have the main body of a report and then an appendix that I want to have a different header or footer, I'd go to the first page of the appendix.

Whichever one it is, you want the first page of the second section.

Once you've clicked into that header or footer, go to the Navigation section of the Headers & Footers Tools Design tab.

You'll see a Link to Previous option that is already selected by default.

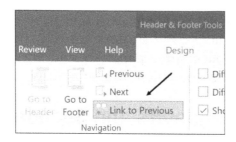

Click on it once to turn it off. It will no longer be highlighted in gray at that point.

Nothing will change when you do this. You will need to edit the header or footer in either or both of the two sections to see a difference.

Page Numbers and Section Breaks

For example, if you need to edit the page numbering of two sections like a table of contents and the main body of the document so that they have different page numbers, you'd need to make edits to the page numbering in both of those sections. In the main body you'd have to turn off the option to continue page numbering from the previous section and in the table of contents section you'd need to change the numbering format.

To change page numbering for a section, highlight a page number from that section, right-click, and choose Format Page Numbers from the dropdown menu. This will bring up the Page Number Format dialogue box. (Your other option is to go to the Header & Footer section of the Header & Footer Tools Design tab, click on the dropdown for Page Number, and choose Format Page Numbers from there. This too will bring up the Page Number Format dialogue box.)

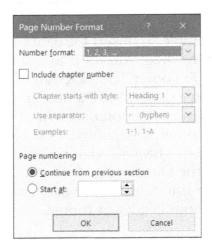

At the top of the dialogue box you can change the style of the numbering. Your choices are 1, 2, 3 as well as i, ii, iii and then some stranger ones like a, b, c and I, II, III as well as one with dashes on either side of the 1, 2, 3.

At the bottom of the dialogue box you can uncheck the box to continue the page numbering from the previous section. The default will then be to start your page numbering for that section at 1 (or i or A, etc.).

You can also set a section to start at any number you want in the Start At field. So if for some reason you were using different Word files for different sections of a report (which you really shouldn't have to do) then you might set this value to 3, 5, or whatever the starting page number for the section needs to be.

So let's step back and look at that table of contents/main body example again and walk through the steps to create two separate sets of page numbers.

First, we'd go to the first page of the main body and unlink that section from the prior section.

Next, we could update the page numbering so that it does not continue from the previous section.

Finally, we could go to the table of contents section and change the number format for that section to i, ii, iii.

At that point all pages in the table of contents section should be numbered i, ii, iii etc. and all pages in the main body should be numbered 1, 2, 3, etc. with the main body section starting at page 1.

(And again, don't worry if you don't do this perfect the first time. I often forget one part or another and have to bounce back and forth between my various headers and footers to get things looking exactly how I want them to. Unless you do this all the time, it can be a bit of trial and error.)

Add Date And/Or Time To Your Header Or Footer

This one is actually pretty simple. To insert the date and/or time into your header or footer, go to the location where you want to insert it (the header or footer), and then go to the Header & Footer Tools Design tab.

(If your document doesn't already have a header or footer and this is all you want to insert, go to the Header & Footer section of the Insert tab, click on the dropdown for Header or Footer, and choose Edit Header or Edit Footer from the bottom of the dropdown. This will open a blank header or footer for you.)

In the Insert section of the Design tab, click on Date & Time. This will bring up a Date & Time dialogue box. Choose the date and/or time format you want and it will be inserted into your header or footer.

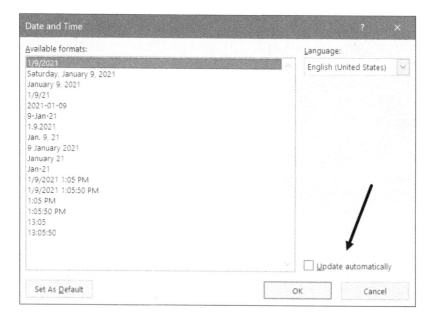

If you want the date and time to update so that it always displays the current date and/or time, be sure to check the box that says Update Automatically in the bottom right corner of the dialogue box.

(Just be sure that's what you really want. I can't count the number of memos I've seen where someone used the automatic date option and shouldn't have. Instead of the memo being dated the day it was actually written and finalized, the memo updated to the current date each time it was opened which can have serious ramifications under certain circumstances.)

Add Document Information or Photos To Your Header Or Footer

You can also have the header or footer include certain document information such as the Author, File Name, File Path, or Document Title.

It works just the same as adding a date or time except you use the Document Info dropdown in the Insert section of the Design tab.

You can choose Author, File Name, File Type, and Document Title from the dropdown menu. There is also a secondary dropdown menu for Document Property that includes fields like company information, publication date, and keywords.

If you want even more information choices, you can click on Field in the dropdown menu to bring up the Field dialogue box which includes a large number of additional fields you probably won't need. SectionPages does allow you to have Page X of Y for a section where Y is the SectionPages value. NumPages will do the same for the entire document.

All of the document information fields are dynamic fields, so will update as the information changes.

The Quick Parts dropdown next to that includes an AutoText option which appears to contain user name and user initials as two more default options.

The final two options in that Insert section are for pictures. This is helpful for if you ever need to include a logo in your header section. Just click on Pictures and then navigate to where your image is stored and select it.

The header or footer will expand to accommodate the image. Click on the round circle in the corner of the image and drag at an angle to resize it to the size you want.

You can also edit the dimensions of the photo in the Picture Tools Format tab that will appear when you insert a photo into the header or footer.

The Picture Tools Format tab also lets you adjust other image attributes. (We'll talk about those attributes more in the section on inserting images into a Word document, because they're the same whether you insert into a header or footer or into the main body of the document.)

Edit Header/Footer Position

By default in Word 2019, the header and footer are positioned .5" from the top and bottom of the page. If you want to change that setting, it's in the Position section of the Header & Footer Tools Design tab.

Edit Header/Footer Text Format

You can edit the formatting of the header or footer text just like you would any text in the main document. You can change the font, font size, font color, alignment, add bolding, italics, or underline, etc.

To do so, select the text you want to change and use the options in the mini formatting menu or the Font section of the Home tab.

You can also select the text you want to change and then right-click and choose Font to pull up the Font dialogue box which has two tabs in this instance, Font and Advanced. Font is for font choice, color, format, etc. Advanced is more for character spacing and things like that you probably won't use often.

You can also choose Paragraph from the dropdown menu to change indents, alignment, line spacing, etc. although, again, not one you're likely to use often.

Footnotes and Endnotes

Since we just talked about headers and footers, let's also talk about footnotes and endnotes.

Footnotes go at the bottom of the page. Endnotes go at the end of the document or the section. Other than that, they're pretty similar in how they work and how you insert them into your document.

To insert a footnote or endnote, click into the point in your main document text where you want to place the note and go to the Footnotes section of the References tab. Click on either Insert Footnote or Insert Endnote.

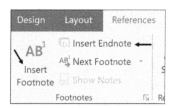

Word will then insert the footnote or endnote number at that point as a superscript number and will add a line either at the bottom of the page or the end of the document and put that same number below the line.

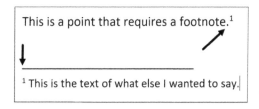

You can then type text next to the number at the bottom of the page or the end of the document like I did above.

The default in Word is for the footnote or endnote to be in 10 pt where the main text is in 11 pt.

If you want to change the font or font size in the note, I recommend updating the style associated with the note so that you only have to make that adjustment once.

To do so, right-click on the text in the note and choose Style from the dropdown menu. This will bring up a Style dialogue box that should have the name of the style already highlighted. Click on Modify to bring up a dialogue box where you can make your changes.

The Footnote and Endnote dialogue box allows for control over the placement of the notes as well as the numbering style for the notes. To access it, click on the expansion arrow in the Footnotes section of the References tab or right-click on the text of a note and choose Note options from the dropdown.

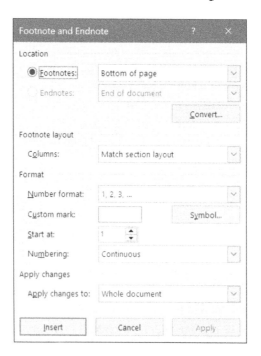

The Location section at the top of the dialogue box lets you determine where the endnote or footnote will be located.

For footnotes your choice is the bottom of the page or below the text. Choosing below the text means that if your text doesn't fill the entire page that the footnote will appear about a line below the text. Choosing bottom of the page means that even if there is only one line of text on a page the footnote will still be at the very bottom of the page.

For endnotes the choice is either to put the endnote at the end of the document or at the end of the section.

The Convert option allows you to turn footnotes into endnotes or endnotes into footnotes with one click. If your document has both you can also choose to swap them so that your footnotes become endnotes and your endnotes become footnotes.

Just click on Convert and then choose the option you want. (Remember that footnotes and endnotes have different styles applied to them if you do this so you may need to edit the style for the note type you're now using.)

The next section, Footnote Layout, lets you decide whether or not to display your footnotes in columns at the bottom of the page. I've seen this done a few times in lengthy non-fiction books with significant amounts of footnotes and small text in general. They kept the main body text in one column, but then had the footnotes in two columns to make it more clear which was which.

You can have up to four columns like I've done here where I also have notes showing below the text instead of at the end of the page.

This is something I wanted to make a subpoint about.[1]

And this is me saying something else to see what happens here with it below the text.[2]

And another point.[3]

And another one.[4]

And another.[5]

---

[1] And this is my additional comment.

[2] More footnotes.
[3] And more and more.

[4] And more.

[5] More and more and more to say.

The Format section below that lets you choose the number format to use. Footnotes default to 1, 2, 3 and endnotes default to i, ii, iii but you can change that.

Custom mark lets you use marks instead of numbers. For example I've seen little daggers and other symbols used as footnote markers before. If you click on Symbol you can choose your desired symbol from the Symbol dialogue box.

When you click on your choice it will be inserted as a new footnote with the symbol you chose inserted at that point in your document as well as in the footnotes section.

The Start At option lets you dictate what number to start your footnotes or endnotes with.

The Numbering option lets you indicate if the numbering should be continuous throughout the document or restart with each section or page.

The final section lets you decide whether to apply your changes to the entire document or just the current section.

To navigate from one footnote or endnote to the next in your document, use the Next Footnote dropdown in the Footnotes section of the References tab.

The Show Notes option in the References tab will move you back and forth between a note and the position in the main body text where that note is used. (This can be very helpful when dealing with endnotes.)

You can also right-click on the text of a note and choose Go to Footnote or Go to Endnote to see the location of the note in the document.

To delete a footnote or endnote from your document, you have to do so in the document itself. Deleting the text of the footnote or endnote will still leave the number in your document. Only selecting and deleting the small superscripted number or symbol from within your main body text will delete the entire footnote or endnote.

Be careful applying styles to the main body text in a document that already has footnotes or endnotes. I tested this with a few different default styles provided by Word and some of them turned the superscript number or symbol used in the text to denote a footnote or endnote into normal text. It doesn't appear that changing the font size or font will do this in Word 2019, but changing the style sometimes did. Once that happened the only way to fix it was to Undo because changing the style back did not put the superscript formatting back.

With respect to track changes, if you have track changes turned on and you edit the text in a footnote or endnote, those edits will be shown in track changes. However, you cannot tie a comment to a footnote or endnote.

Also, when you're reading a document, if you want to see what the text of a footnote or endnote is without going to the actual note, you can do so by holding your cursor over the number in the text and it will appear as a note. But if you were working in track changes the text that appears is both the deleted and current text, as you can see in the example below.

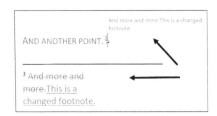

Conclusion

Alright, so that was the basics of page formatting in Word 2019. If you get stuck, reach out and I'm happy to help if I can. I don't check email every day, but I do check it regularly.

Good luck with it.

And if you decide that you want to learn more about Microsoft Word or Word 2019, feel free to check out my other books.

Appendix A: Basic Terminology

Below are some basic terms that I use throughout this guide.

Tab

I refer to the menu choices at the top of the screen (File, Home, Insert, Design, Layout, References, Mailings, Review, View, and Help) as tabs.

Click

If I tell you to click on something, that means to use your mouse (or trackpad) to move the arrow on the screen over to a specific location and left-click or right-click on the option. If I don't specify which to use, left-click.

Select or Highlight

If I tell you to select text, that means to highlight that text either by using your mouse or the arrow and shift keys. Selected text is highlighted in gray.

Dropdown Menu

A dropdown menu provides you a list of choices to select from. There are dropdown menus when you right-click in your document workspace as well as for some of the options listed under the tabs at the top of the screen. Each option with a small arrow next to it will have a dropdown menu available.

Expansion Arrows

I refer to the little arrows at the bottom right corner of most of the sections in each tab as expansion arrows. For example, click on the expansion arrow in the Clipboard section of the Home tab and it will open the Clipboard task pane.

Dialogue Box

Dialogue boxes are pop-up boxes that cover specialized settings. They allow the most granular level of control over an option.

Scroll Bar

Scroll bars are on the right-hand side of the workspace and sometimes along the bottom. They allow you to scroll through your document if your text takes up more space than you can see in the workspace.

Arrow

If I ever tell you to arrow to the left or right or up or down, that just means use your arrow keys.

Task Pane

I refer to the panes that sometimes appear to the left, right, and bottom of the main workspace as task panes. By default you should see the Navigation task pane on the left-hand side when you open a new document in Word.

Control Shortcut

I'll occasionally mention control shortcuts that you can use to perform tasks. When I reference them I'll do so by writing it as Ctrl + a capital letter. For example, Save is Ctrl + S.

To use one, hold down the Ctrl key and the letter at the same time.

ABOUT THE AUTHOR

M.L. Humphrey is a former stockbroker with a degree in Economics from Stanford and an MBA from Wharton who has spent close to twenty years as a regulator and consultant in the financial services industry.

You can reach M.L. Humphrey at:

mlhumphreywriter@gmail.com

or at

www.mlhumphrey.com

www.ingramcontent.com/pod-product-compliance
Lightning Source LLC
Chambersburg PA
CBHW060512060326

40689CB00020B/4714